Made in the USA
Coppell, TX
13 May 2020

25540774R00056